small steps *for* catholic moms

COMPANION JOURNAL

Danielle Bean & Elizabeth Foss

FAITH & FAMILY
BOOKS
An Imprint of Circle Press | CirclePress.org

FAITH & FAMILY
BOOKS
An Imprint of Circle Press | CirclePress.org

Published by Circle Press, a division of Circle Media, Inc.

ISBN 978-1-933271-39-2

PRINTED IN THE UNITED STATES OF AMERICA

8 7 6 5 4 3 2

FIRST EDITION

Table of Contents

JANUARY

Joy

Sometimes finding joy is simply a matter of slowing down enough to notice it.

After Mass one November day, we stopped at a local high school to check out the new track and football field they had recently built. When we pulled up in the van and opened the doors, the kids leaped joyfully from their seats and ran onto the field.

Where do they get that kind of natural enthusiasm? The baby was napping, so instead of joining them, I stayed in the van and watched.

The air was cold, but the sky was clear and the midday sun shone brightly down upon my gang of shouting children. Their winter coats splashed blue, red, and orange against the bright green field and cloudless sky.

The big boys sprinted side by side for the full 100 yards and then fell laughingly to the turf. Juliette hiked up her skirt a bit and skipped cheerfully in the open air as Gabrielle galloped along behind. An icy wind whipped through Gabby's hair and swallowed her gleeful shouts, but I could see her small face, grinning and glowing in the bright sun.

Raphael was the littlest one, a small dot of navy blue on the opposite end of the field. I watched as he raised one arm above his head, gave a yell, and began to run. His legs worked steadily, scampering along behind his brothers. Small arms pumped purposefully at his sides. As he came closer, I could make out more clearly the details of his face. His eyes squinted in the sun. His mouth was open—panting, shouting, laughing.

I know the joy of heaven knows no earthly comparison. But on days like this, I can't help but wonder if it might feel a little bit like cool wind warmed by sunshine. Or if it might sound something like a joyful shout carried across an open field and look a little like a small girl's wind-whipped hair, tousled and tangled. Or if it might taste like a boy's sun-kissed face, fresh and flushed, when he climbs back into the van and hugs me.

— *Danielle Bean*

On Your Own

1. What kinds of things bring you joy without effort? Make a list of the joyful moments you encounter on a daily basis.

____

____

____

____

____

____

2. Ask God to show you ways that you can better cultivate joy in your day-to-day moments. Ask God to help

you know the difference between joy and happiness or pleasure. Write these down.

____

____

____

____

____

____

3. Look outside yourself. Is there someone you know who needs more joy in his or her life? What prevents you from spreading joy to others? What can you do to remove those obstacles this month?

____

____

____

____

____

____

For Further Discussion

1. *"In the family, women have the opportunity to transmit the faith in the early training of their children. They are particularly responsible for the joyful task of leading them to discover the supernatural world" (Pope John Paul II).* How can we intentionally encourage our children, grandchildren, or godchildren to discover the joy of their faith? What kinds of experiences did you have growing up or did you see in other families that contributed to a sense of joy about the faith?

2. Read Isaiah 55: 10-12. What are some ways that the natural world instills in you a sense of joy and draws you closer to God?

---

3. Drawing upon the essay, your journaling, and the discussion, what resolution can you make this month with regard to joy? Choose one quotation from the book or from your journal this month and commit it to memory so that you can draw upon it as you work toward joy.

Extra Space for Journaling

FEBRUARY

Simplicity

My life is not simple. My life is complex. I am responsible for the care and nurturing of ten other people. They live under my roof. I feed them and clothe them and counsel them and pray for them. When they are sick, I nurse them back to health. Ten people. There is no way that can be simple.

I can try to make the running of my household simple. I can try to pin down that elusive system that forces everything to march in a perfectly orderly manner so that it all looks sleek and uncluttered as an Amish kitchen, but sooner or later I will be frustrated to learn yet again that there is no simple system that will work here. Even if each component is simple, the big picture is a complex tapestry.

Sometimes, particularly when I'm tired, I wish everything was simple. But then I usually quickly recognize that I'm wishing away the very life for which I prayed. I begged God for the fascinating, complex man who is my husband. I begged God for every single one of these children. I begged God for the means to buy them the clothes that necessitate nearly perpetual sorting, washing, folding, and putting away. I begged God for the good job my husband holds which provides ample food that requires extensive planning, shopping, cooking, and serving (and also means an erratic work schedule and frequent travel). I begged God for this house, for the things in it, which he has so graciously provided and which I must clean and maintain.

But none of it is simple. Not a single bit of it.

The only simple part is how I do it. I am called to do it diligently. I am called to do it wholeheartedly. I am called to devote my entire life to working hard for the glory of God in this complex household. I am called to do it—no matter how intricate and complicated "it" is—with love.

Mother Teresa lived a life of seeming simplicity. But was it really simple? She founded an order, traveled the globe, fed millions, saved lives, dined with heads of state, worked for the kingdom of God. This was a rich and complex woman, a deeply spiritual woman. And, I think, what made it all seem like a simple life was her agenda. At the root of everything, all she wanted was to love.

Today I am off to spend the day in an increasingly familiar circuit of orthopedist and physical therapist, grocery store and post office. I'll come home to cooking and cleaning and laundry and maybe a little bit of writing.

I sat last night and mapped it all out—I had to in order to be sure that I did the work that is mine for the day. It all looks a bit messy on my handwritten list. It looks absolutely nothing like I thought it would at the beginning of the week.

Now I give it all to God—the simple part and the overwhelming part. I tell him I will do the very best I can and I trust him to show me what's important, to make his will clear, and to conduct the rich and joyful symphony that is my not-so-simple life.

—*Elizabeth Foss*

On Your Own

1. Make a thoughtful list of the biggest things that threaten to complicate your life (meals, laundry, carpooling, work, etc.), even if they are a part of your primary vocation.

2. Ask God to show you how the items on your list differ from your calling to be simple-hearted. How can you maintain an interior simplicity, even if your daily life is full of complications?

____

____

____

____

____

____

3. Make a commitment to simplify your surroundings. What kind of physical stuff are you holding on to? What things could you do away with this month to create an uncluttered work environment?

____

____

____

____

For Further Discussion

1. *"I just take one day. Yesterday is gone. Tomorrow has not come. We have only today to love Jesus" (Blessed Teresa of Calcutta).*

Do you find it difficult to focus on just today? Do you tend to focus on the past or the future in the place of the present? What are some ways that we can help ourselves and one another focus on the task at hand, with simple hearts?

2. *"Gracious is the Lord and just; yes, our God is merciful. The Lord protects the simple; I was helpless, but God saved me. Return, my soul, to your rest; the Lord has been good to you. For my soul has been freed from death, my eyes from tears, my feet from stumbling. I shall walk before the Lord in the land of the living" (Psalm 116: 5-9).*

Discuss how this psalm helps us put all of our daily worries and complications into perspective. Share some times in your life where you could see clearly that, in spite of how complicated it seemed, God really did have a simple plan for you.

____

____

____

____

____

____

____

____

3. Drawing upon the essay, your journaling, and the discussion, what resolution can you make this month with regard to simplicity? Choose one quotation from the book or from your journal this month and commit it to memory so that you can draw upon it as you work toward simplicity.

Extra Space for Journaling

MARCH

Sacrifice

I never intended to be a "family bed" type. Where my children sleep is not an issue I take any kind of political stance on. It's just kind of something that has happened to me. Without my consent, even.

A couple of years ago, almost every night, my baby boys would sandwich me. It was not always a comfortable sandwich, but it was a predictable one. Daniel, thoroughly spoiled, nursed on and off throughout the night.

At some point after midnight, Raphael also used to find his way to my bed. He would snuggle in behind me and press his small body against my back. He smoothed my hair, patted my head, and nuzzled the back of my neck.

The boys were agreeable enough. Unless I tried to move, that is. This was a coercive sandwich, after all. Mama was not permitted to move.

But sometimes I needed to. I remember one particularly trying night, when I had one vomiting older child and another with a bad case of nightmares. Every time I shimmied my way out from between the two babies, however, a howl of protest rose from the bed.

This happened several times before, "This is ridiculous," some exhausted person finally was heard to say. Perhaps even loudly enough to wake her husband (how do they sleep through these things?).

It was ridiculous. And yet, simply because I was so tired, that night I did not fight the sandwich.

And so it was that at 4:00 in the morning I found myself—worn out and yet wide awake—squashed between babies. As I cradled Daniel with one arm and reached awkwardly behind me to pat my enormous toddler with the other, I smiled at how closely my circumstances reflected the ridiculousness of an everyday reality.

I suffer from an absurdity of abundance. Always stretched to my limit. And always blessed without limit.

—Danielle Bean

On Your Own

1. Write out a list of the things you tend to complain about, even if only in your own thoughts.

2. Look over your list and prayerfully consider the fact that by putting you where you are right now, God might be calling you to make more willing sacrifices in those areas.

____

____

____

____

____

____

____

____

____

____

3. Make a positive move toward changing your attitude toward your particular areas of sacrifice. When you find yourself beginning to grumble, change your words from complaint to: "Thank you, God, for this opportunity to grow."

For Further Discussion

1. *"Oh what a pity it is to see some souls, like rich ships, loaded with a precious freight of good works, spiritual exercises, virtues and favors from God, which, for want of courage to make an end of some miserable little fancy or affection, can never arrive at the port of divine union, while it only needs one good earnest effort to break asunder that thread of attachment!" (St. John Chrysostom)*

Many of us are very good about giving up things of our own choosing, but might God be calling you to give up something else that you are attached to? In what areas of your life do you struggle with wanting personal control as opposed to giving God control? Once you recognize that you are being called to make a certain sacrifice in your life, how can you go about doing it cheerfully? Who are some people who inspire you with their example of cheerful sacrifice?

2. *"There is an appointed time for everything, and a time for every affair under the heavens" (Ecclesiastes 3:1).*

Think about the season of motherhood you are in right now. What kinds of sacrifices—even unusual or unexpected ones—are a natural part of that season? What are some ways women can support other women in the particular sacrifices they are required to make as wives and mothers?

3. Drawing upon the essay, your journaling, and the discussion, what resolution can you make this month with regard to sacrifice? Choose one quotation from the book or from your journal this month and commit it to memory so that you can draw upon it as you work toward sacrifice.

APRIL

Courage

I think back to times in my past when I was a little girl undergoing one surgery after another to construct an ear that was never there, a young mother facing chemotherapy and uncertainty, and a mother of many warned by doctors that she could die delivering the baby she carried.

In each instance, people commended my courage. But those weren't instances of courage to me. They were just doing what had to be done.

Courage was what I'd beg of God when I just couldn't keep breathing on my own, when my breath caught and I needed God just to exhale. Courage was my prayer when I let my teenagers go out into that great big world. What I wanted was to keep them home, hold them close, protect them forever.

As my big boys began to march forth into life, they walked around with pieces of my heart inside of them. Suddenly, I was vulnerable. I saw that they were going to be hurt and I was going to watch them suffer. There was no way around it. They would make mistakes and get hurt. They would learn about what's out there in a fallen world and get hurt. They would meet many people and some of them would hurt them.

Nothing was ever so simple as it was when they were babies in my arms. Then, I could gather them up and soothe their hurts, chase away their fears, make every little thing "all better" just by my presence. But as they grew, I found myself praying for courage. I began to understand that, for mothers, the heroic effort is in letting them go.

It's not so much that I wanted my children to be little again. To want that would have been to wish away the beautiful people they had grown to be, to wish away years of loving and living together.

No, instead, I wanted to be the mother I was when they were babies. I wanted the power to gather them on my lap and soothe them as I rocked. I wanted to shelter and protect and to be their whole world. I wanted to be able to ensure that their days were happy and healthy and holy. I wanted to cradle them in the protection of my arms. I wanted to love them with all my heart. And I wanted that to be enough. Instead, I must remember that for all their lives, my calling is to have the courage to love them, knowing that they will leave, and trusting that God will care for them more tenderly than I ever could.

Mothering older children takes courage, because just as sure as the sun will rise, so will there be trouble in the lives of our children. I am left to storm heaven on their behalf and to thank the Lord for the gift they are.

I shore myself up for the years of mothering that lie ahead by reminding myself of the words of Blessed Mary MacKillop: "Whatever troubles may be before you, accept them bravely, remembering whom you are trying to follow. Do not be afraid. Love one another, bear with one another, and let charity guide you all your life. God will reward you as only he can."

—*Elizabeth Foss*

On Your Own

1. Prayerfully consider those things of which you are afraid. Make a conscious decision to turn your fears over to God, knowing that he is more powerful and more capable and more loving than you could ever hope to be.

____

____

____

____

____

2. When you hold your fears tightly in your hands, all control slips away anyway. Ask God to give you the gift of courage to put your hand in his and step out in trust. Write down a one-sentence prayer that you can pray when doubt and worry creep in and distract.

3. Concentrate on one of your biggest fears. Think of a small step you can take towards facing that fear. Step out in faith and work toward crossing that fear off your list.

____

____

____

____

____

____

For Further Discussion

1. *"In dangers, in doubts, in difficulties, think of Mary, call upon Mary. Let not her name depart from your lips, never suffer it to leave your heart. And that you may obtain the assistance of her prayer, neglect not to walk in her footsteps. With her for a guide, you shall never go astray; while invoking her, you shall never lose heart; so long as*

she is in your mind, you are safe from deception; while she holds your hand, you cannot fall; under her protection you have nothing to fear; if she walks before you, you shall not grow weary; if she shows you favor, you shall reach the goal" (St. Bernard of Clairvaux).

In what ways can you keep Mary before you as a model of faith over fear? How does her fiat inspire our faith? Can we encourage each other to be courageous and hold each other accountable as we seek to be faithful, not fearful?

2. *"Now who is going to harm you if you are enthusiastic for what is good? But even if you should suffer because of righteousness, blessed are you. Do not be afraid or terrified with fear of them, but sanctify Christ as Lord in your hearts. Always be ready to give an explanation to anyone who asks you for a reason for your hope, but do it with gentleness and reverence, keeping your conscience clear, so that, when you are maligned, those who defame your good conduct in Christ may themselves be put to shame. For it is better to suffer for doing good, if that be the will of God, than for doing evil" (1 Peter 3:13-17).*

Are you afraid to give wholehearted assent to the will of God? Is there an area of faith that you fear? For instance, can you be wholeheartedly open to life? Are you able to courageously encourage your children to consider a vocation to the priesthood or consecrated life? Can you trust God's providence in areas of finance and material needs?

____

____

____

3. Drawing upon the essay, your journaling, and the discussion, what resolution can you make this month with regard to courage? Choose one quotation from the book or from your journal this month and commit it to memory so that you can draw upon it as you work toward courage.

Extra Space for Journaling

MAY

Grace

This morning, I locked myself in my bedroom to steal a few minutes of quiet while I typed an e-mail.

When two-year-old Daniel knocked on the door, whining, I took pity on him and opened the door. That was a mistake.

He leaped onto the bed and lunged for the alarm clock, switching on the radio with a single slap of his hand. Where did he learn to do that?

Gwen Stefani filled the room.

Seconds later, Raphael noticed the open door and settled on the floor with a pile of clothing next to him. Despite the fact that it was mid-morning, he had not yet gotten dressed for the day.

"Nobody wook!" he announced, pulling on a shirt and undies.

Next, Juliette entered the room with a spelling list in hand. I put aside my e-mail to quiz her. We had been working hard on this list and I wanted to be sure she had mastered it before moving on to other subjects for the morning.

Finally, Stephen wandered in. With a singing stuffed hamster. Yes, you read that right.

In fact, I would like to take this opportunity to publicly thank Father David, my husband's boss, for sending this small gift home with him two years ago. It's a six-inch-tall stuffed hamster that dances and sings a lively rendition of "Wide Blue Yonder" when you squeeze its paw. And it never runs out of batteries. Not ever.

The hamster's voice blended melodically with Gwen Stefani's. I called out spelling words above the din and wondered if I would manage to send that e-mail after all.

But it didn't matter anyway. This is what working at home, schooling at home, living and loving at home look and sound like.

This is not at all what I imagined my daily life would be like. How could I have envisioned this?

But this, I find, is how God's grace works. It's not always easy. It's not always pretty. But it is everything to me. Everything I should be doing, everything I want to be doing, everything I need.

—Danielle Bean

On Your Own

1. If you see your life as a tapestry woven by God, what are the individual strands of grace woven by God? Write down some different aspects of your life—even ones that trouble you or are not what you had in mind—that could be God's grace at work in your life.

___

___

___

___

2. Taking some of the "messy" details from your list, pray about ways to see those things from God's perspective. What might be the "bigger picture" with regard to those little things that God sees and you do not?

3. One of the greatest sources of grace we have on earth is access to regular confession. When was the last time you went? What's holding you back?

____

____

____

____

____

For Further Discussion

1. *"Let the soul of Mary be in each of us to magnify the Lord and the spirit of Mary be in each of us to rejoice in God" (St. Ambrose).*

Mary is "full of grace." She is our model and our source of God's grace. What are some ways that we can imitate Mary's openness to God's grace so that we make ourselves more open to God's grace? How might modeling our lives after Mary and being open to grace bring us joy every moment—even when we're not "happy?"

___

___

___

___

___

___

___

___

___

2. *"Therefore, that I might not become too elated, a thorn in the flesh was given to me, an angel of Satan, to beat me, to keep me from being too elated. Three times I begged the Lord about this, that it might leave me, but he said to me, "My grace is sufficient for you, for power is made perfect in weakness." I will rather boast most gladly of my weaknesses, in order that the power of Christ may dwell with me. There-*

fore, I am content with weaknesses, insults, hardships, persecutions, and constraints, for the sake of Christ; for when I am weak, then I am strong" (2 Corinthians 12:7).

What are some ways that our weaknesses help us grow closer to God and increase our awareness of our dependence on him?

____

____

____

____

____

____

____

____

____

____

____

____

____

3. Drawing upon the essay, your journaling, and the discussion, what resolution can you make this month with regard to being open to God's grace? Choose one quotation from the book or from your journal this month and commit it to memory so that you can draw upon it as you work toward being more open to grace.

Extra Space for Journaling

JUNE

Gentleness

Often, when I look for ways to inspire virtue in my children, I find instead that virtue is inspired in me first. Such was the case when I searched for St. Jean Vianney quotes for my children to ponder during the summer of the Year for Priests.

St. Jean Vianney piqued my interest immediately by pointing to the example of a favorite saint. He wrote, "St. Francis de Sales, that great saint, would leave off writing with the letter of a word half-formed in order to reply to an interruption." Hey, Elizabeth, saints don't say, "Just a minute," and then finish writing the sentence or the paragraph or the entire post or project while toddlers melt down and little boys wrestle. They leave the letters half-formed.

Since neither St. Jean Vianney nor St. Francis de Sales was a mother who worked at home, it probably wasn't little girls with big blue eyes and crazy curls who interrupted them. No, they probably put their pen down for older people, people who really could wait. People who didn't pretty much depend on them for the whole world. But my small people depend on me for everything and still I sometimes see them as interruptions.

Surely children must learn to wait; I don't dispute that fact. Often, though, adults must learn to stop and see the child and to respond with careful attention and thoughtful gentleness. Children can teach us to be present in the moment. They can require us to slow down and truly listen, because, frankly, no one can readily understand a two-year-old without focusing and looking at context and listening carefully and asking clarifying questions. No one can listen to a two-year-old with absentminded attention while attempting to multitask and really understand what the child is saying. And neither mother nor child grows in virtue if interruptions are met with anger.

Children can teach us gentleness, if only we have teachable spirits. Gentle mothers make an effort to speak softly and less often, to listen carefully and more often. Mothers who are able to permeate the atmosphere of their homes with gentleness can see God's hand when a child interrupts her work. Like the monastery bell calls a monk, the child calls a mother to service, and her work with the child becomes a prayer. If she is wise, she will see opportunity to grow in holiness in every interruption. She will count every call to gentleness over exasperation a blessing.

Father John Hardon reminded us, "Gentleness is the virtue that restrains the passion of anger. Over the centuries it has been variously described—sometimes poetically, sometimes theologically. Where anger flares up, gentleness calms down. Where anger is a bursting flame, gentleness is a gentle rain. Where anger asserts itself and crushes, gentleness embraces and quiets and soothes. Yet as we hear these and similar descriptions of gentleness, we are liable to make the mistake I dare say so much of the modern world makes—the mistake of identifying gentleness with weakness."

It is not a weak woman who is gentle when her home is bustling with activity and several people are dependent upon her for their very existence. It is a strong woman who gathers the grace necessary to respond with goodness and gentleness and brings peace to her family. This summer, I pray for the strength to be gentle.

—Elizabeth Foss

On Your Own

1. Think about what your natural response usually is when you are interrupted. Write down some of the ways—both positive and negative—that you tend to react when interrupted. Include different responses you have to different kinds of interruptions (from children, from husband, from messes).

____

____

____

____

____

____

____

____

2. Pray about how you look at interruptions in your daily life. Ask God to help you see what kinds of "interruptions" you have in your life that are actually part of your primary work.

____

____

____

____

3. Encourage and remind yourself to be gentle as you go about your daily round. Light a candle or wear a special bracelet that will serve as a reminder to be more

gentle in your daily routine. When you notice your reminder, quiet your tone and calm your actions.

____

____

____

____

____

For Further Discussion

1. *"The insight of the most skilled doctors can't compare to a mother's heart" (St. Therese of Lisieux).*

Do you fully recognize the power you have as a mother? Share some ways that you have seen the power of a mother's gentle strength empower her family. Talk about how confident children, happy husbands, peaceful homes all begin with a strong, gentle woman.

____

____

____

____

____

____

____

____

2. *"Rejoice in the Lord always. I shall say it again: rejoice! Your kindness should be known to all. The Lord is near. Have no anxiety at all, but in everything, by prayer and petition, with thanksgiving, make your requests known to God. Then the peace of God that surpasses all understanding will guard your hearts and minds in Christ Jesus. Finally, brothers, whatever is true, whatever is honorable, whatever is just, whatever is pure, whatever is lovely, whatever is gracious, if there is any excellence and if there is anything worthy of praise, think about these things. Keep on doing what you have learned and received and*

heard and seen in me. Then the God of peace will be with you" (Philippians 4:4-9).

Mary's entire life was a witness to this kind of gentle strength and confidence in God. What are some ways that a modern-day wife and mother can model her life after Mary's example of gentleness and strength?

____

____

____

____

____

____

____

____

____

3. Drawing upon the essay, your journaling, and the discussion, what resolution can you make this month with regard to gentleness? Choose one quotation from the

book or from your journal this month and commit it to memory so that you can draw upon it as you work toward gentleness.

JULY

Humility

'Tis the season. Schedules are looser. Children run through the neighborhood, moving freely from one house to another. At any given moment, someone just might drop in unannounced. I try not to let my perfectionist panic set in. Breathing deeply, I pray that God will show me how to entertain with grace this summer.

The Holy Spirit offers an alternative that saves my sanity and offers sanctity. Instead of entertaining, I will focus on hospitality. The differences are not subtle. When we entertain, we are often ruled by our pride. When we offer hospitality, we are infused with humility and inspired by charity.

A true ministry, hospitality is not bound by time or space. To offer hospitality, I do not have to offer an invitation; I do not even have to be at home and I certainly do not need to spend days beforehand cooking and cleaning and decorating. To offer hospitality, I open my heart to see and meet a need. Hospitality might be a home-cooked meal wrapped in a pretty towel and carried, still warm, to a neighbor who is going through a difficult time.

The charity of an open home extended to a child while his mother has a moment to herself is hospitality extended to all. The comfort of a friend who offers a cup of tea at a well-worn kitchen table on a teary afternoon is hospitality that cannot be captured on the glossy pages of a magazine.

In order to be truly hospitable, I must put away pride. I must be willing to open my doors, no matter the state of my home or my wardrobe, and to graciously seek to make visitors feel at ease. In all humility, I have to let people to see me as I am. I have to put away pretense and offer myself with all my weaknesses. They can see me strive humbly towards holiness and fall short and they can see that only God can perfect me. When I offer myself to other people and allow them to see my imperfection, I take a chance.

We hope that they, too, will accept me in a spirit of charity. Hospitality works best when both the giver and the receiver assume the best about each other.

Entertaining often has a reward attached to it: social stature, an accolade, a return invitation. Hospitality is freely-given, with no thought to reciprocity or reward. The heart that is ordered towards charity offers hospitality to those who most need it, even if those are not the people whose company we most desire. This is charity—a virtue we can model for our children when we ensure that they are hospitable to their friends and even to the child who might otherwise be excluded.

As we begin to practice the ministry of hospitality, we allow ourselves to be vulnerable. The most hospitable of us are the humblest. We open our doors and our hearts and certainly some people will come through those doors who don't view our efforts through the same lens of charity. On occasion, we will hear a critical comment; we will be judged according to the world's standards. We will feel as if we've come up short. But we haven't truly. Those are the times the hospitable hostess will offer to Christ, imperfect and heartfelt, knowing that he will redeem the time and the effort.

—Elizabeth Foss

On Your Own

1. How do feelings of insecurity or vulnerability keep you from ministering to your neighbor? Make a list of places where you could be fully open to meeting the needs of others if only you were humble enough to let go of caring what people will think.

____

____

____

2. Bring your list to God in prayer and ask him to show you which of these items he'd most want you to focus on this month. Have a conversation with God and be open to the fruits of the Holy Spirit's promptings.

3. Make a practical plan. Now that you have sense of what God wants from you, think of some small steps you can take towards serving others with an open heart in the immediate future. Start today!

For Further Discussion

1. *"We certainly are sparks! This is why you want us to humble ourselves. Just as sparks receive their being from the fire, so let us acknowledge that our being comes from our first source" (St. Catherine of Siena).*

Every good thing we do comes from God; we are all just agents of God's grace for other people. Do you think about yourself that way? Thinking about our own importance can impede us and keep us from recognizing ourselves as a tool in God's hands. Share how a change in perspective can help us overcome prideful obstacles like vanity and perfectionism and open us to the fruits of humility.

2. *If there is any encouragement in Christ, any solace in love, any participation in the Spirit, any compassion and mercy, complete my joy by being of the same mind, with the same love, united in heart, thinking one thing. Do nothing out of selfishness or out of vainglory; rather, humbly regard others as more important than yourselves, each looking out not for his own interests, but [also] everyone for those of others. Have among yourselves the same attitude that is also yours in Christ Jesus, Who, though he was in the form of God, did not regard equality with God something to be grasped. Rather, he emptied himself, taking the form of a slave, coming in human likeness; and found human in appearance, he humbled himself, becoming obedient to death, even death on a cross. Because of this, God greatly exalted him and*

bestowed on him the name that is above every name, that at the name of Jesus every knee should bend, of those in heaven and on earth and under the earth, and every tongue confess that Jesus Christ is Lord, to the glory of God the Father" (Phil 2:1-11).

What are some of the most challenging ways that mothers in particular are called to model Christ-like humility in their family lives? How can women of faith support and encourage one another in that calling?

___

___

___

___

___

___

___

___

___

___

3. Drawing upon the essay, your journaling, and the discussion, what resolution can you make this month with regard to humility? Choose one quotation from the book or from your journal this month and commit it to memory so that you can draw upon it as you work toward humility.

Extra Space for Journaling

AUGUST

Charity

Years ago, when we were newlyweds, I struggled to find full-time work while Dan was still a grad student. I wound up taking a temporary job as a waitress in a seafood restaurant to pay the bills.

Soon after I began working there, I discovered I was pregnant. And sick. So very sick.

I still don't why they call it morning sickness, but I am convinced it was a man who named it. For many of us who suffer from it, it's not morning sickness. It's not feel-a-little-queasy-in-the-morning-but-get-over-it-by-noontime sickness. It's all day, all night, every waking moment sickness.

But I needed to work. So between bouts of vomiting, I somehow managed to brush my hair into a ponytail, put on my polyester uniform, pretend my face wasn't green, and show up for work.

I got along all right for a while. But finally, when I had to serve an order of shrimp scampi, I fell apart. The strong odors of shrimp, garlic, butter, and parmesan cheese that wafted from the platter as I carried the large tray from the kitchen positively overwhelmed me. I set the tray down on the nearest surface and raced for the ladies' room.

One of my fellow waitresses, an older woman named Mary, noticed me. She later cornered me in the kitchen and asked me what was wrong. When I poured out my tearful tale of sickness and scampi, she took pity on me.

Immediately, she rearranged the schedule so that the two of us would work most of our shifts together and instructed me to let her know if I needed her to help me in any way. She switched our section assignments so that I never had to work in or near the smoking section. She even took a few of my weekday lunch shifts that no one wanted to work and told me to stay home and nap during those times instead. She made certain that I always got the easy side work jobs, like refilling ketchup bottles, while she took on scrubbing trays in the kitchen, vacuuming, and cleaning the bathrooms.

And this is how true charity works, I have come to realize. It responds immediately. It doesn't demand "fairness," and it doesn't hold back.

Please God, help me to make charity something I don't just practice on special occasions but something I live and breathe and do and am. Every minute of every day.

—Danielle Bean

On Your Own

1. The first step toward charity is noticing the needs of others. What are some of the needs of others—in your home, in your family, or in your community—that you have noticed or could make a greater effort to notice?

2. There are stages in our life where we are able to perform great works of charity outside our homes and there are stages in our lives where the greatest need for our time and attention is within our homes. Prayerfully look over your list. Ask God to keep you quiet, content, and charitable at home if that is where he is calling you to be right now, and to nudge you toward greater charity outside your home if that is where you need to grow.

3. No matter what you discern your place is in life right now, make a commitment to greater charity inside or outside your home. Decide on some daily action you can take that will move you closer to meeting the needs of others. Commit to turning that action into a habit as you work toward greater charity this month.

For Further Discussion

1. *"Be kind and merciful. Let no one ever come to you without coming away better and happier. Be the living expression of God's kindness" (Blessed Teresa of Calcutta).*

All of us have hard days where it would be laughable to call ourselves a "living expression of God's kindness." Share about some of your "bad days." What caused them? What prevented you from turning to God in hard times and made you less than a model of charity?

____

____

____

____

____

____

____

____

2. *"If I speak in human and angelic tongues but do not have love, I am a resounding gong or a clashing cymbal. And if I have the gift of prophecy and comprehend all mysteries and all knowledge; if I have all faith so as to move mountains, but do not have love, I am nothing. If I give away everything I own, and if I hand my body over so that I may boast but do not have love, I gain nothing. Love is patient, love is kind. It is not jealous, [love] is not pompous, it is not inflated, it is not rude, it does not seek its own interests, it is not quick-tempered, it does not brood over injury, it does not rejoice over wrongdoing but rejoices with the truth. It bears all things, believes all things, hopes all things, endures all things. Love never fails. If there are prophecies, they will be brought to nothing; if tongues, they will cease; if knowledge, it will be brought to nothing. For we know partially and we prophesy partially, but when the perfect comes, the partial will pass away. When I was a child, I used to talk as a child, think as a child, reason as a child; when I became a man, I put aside childish things.*

At present we see indistinctly, as in a mirror, but then face to face. At present I know partially; then I shall know fully, as I am fully known. So faith, hope, love remain, these three; but the greatest of these is love" (1 Cor 13: 1-13).

Go through the above Scripture passage above, replacing each instance of the word "love" with your name. Are there any parts that make you cringe? Share your thoughts with the group and see if there might some universal ways in which women have difficulty expressing charity. What are some ways women can build each other up and encourage each other as they work toward greater charity?

___

___

___

___

___

___

___

___

3. Drawing upon the essay, your journaling, and the discussion, what resolution can you make this month with regard to charity? Choose one quotation from the book or from your journal this month and commit it to memory so that you can draw upon it as you work toward charity.

SEPTEMBER

Diligence

My son Michael must have been about twelve years old when he found a quote in an article about Hristo Stoitchkov, an international soccer superstar. He transcribed it, printed it, and taped it to his bedroom wall.

"'Soccer is very, very hard. You must prepare every day,' he said, just as he tells his teammates. 'You must not waste a day… prepare. The game is only ninety minutes. It is nothing. It is over like this' —he snapped his fingers. 'You must work the whole week. Monday, one step. Tuesday, second step. Every single day, step by step. It is impossible for good training Monday, then cheat on Tuesday and Wednesday. Good training Thursday. Nothing Friday. Impossible to win the game Saturday. No. Every single day, I bring water to the tree. One day, I pick the fruit'" (Hristo Stoitchkov in *The Washington Post,* October 24, 2003).

This quote shaped Michael's middle school years, his high school years, his future. He was focused. He was determined. He was diligent. Michael called me this morning to tell me that he's been named the captain of his university's soccer team. He's not the most gifted player, not by a long shot. He's spent far more time on the bench than on the pitch these past two years.

To be a captain is an honor and a responsibility. This is not an accolade awarded to him because he's a superstar defensive back. No, this captaincy is a tribute to his work ethic. He is diligent—over his training, over his academics, even over his teammates. He's a leader and he inspires diligence in everyone around him.

I shake myself, remembering all those nights under stadium lights in the rain, taking shots on goal, all those times I heard the clang of weights in his room long after I thought he was asleep. I am humbled by the example of a child who would forego brownies in favor of fruit because "nutrition isn't just a game day thing." Too often, I live with a game day mentality.

I see the work of my day, laid out before me. I want the whole house to be clean. I envision a good meal on the table every night. There is a book to be written, a column deadline to be met. Those are my game-day goals. How do I get from the ambitious to-do list to the peace that comes at the end of a day well-lived? Perhaps I take a page from the soccer star's playbook, an inspiration from the life of a dedicated student athlete.

What if I could see every day, every moment, as an irreplaceable opportunity to move closer to the goal? I start with one toilet a time, one thoughtful grocery list, one quiet early morning after another at the keyboard. What if I approach each day with diligence? With God as my helper, I can "just do it" every single day, every single moment, knowing that I can't expect to get to "well done" unless I am diligent over the small steps between here and there. No step can be delayed or overlooked or done halfheartedly.

Each day has its own work; each moment seeks to be sanctified by cheerful obedience, by diligence to the task at hand. Game on!

—*Elizabeth Foss*

On Your Own

1. For all of us, heaven is our ultimate goal. List three smaller, long-term goals in your life.

____

____

____

____

____

2. Think about the small steps it takes on a daily basis to work toward the goals you have written down. Think of some concrete things you can do on any given day to work toward those goals.

3. Buy a planner or a notebook—commit to writing a simple plan for incorporating your short-term goals in your daily plans, beginning with this month.

____

____

____

____

____

For Further Discussion

1. *"I have seen through experience the great good that comes to a soul when it does not turn aside from obedience. It is through this practice that I think one advances in virtue and gains humility" (St. Teresa of Avila).*

Not obeying God immediately is the same thing as disobedience. When we know what God's will is for us, we should act upon it immediately. What are your personal obstacles to obeying God immediately in your life?

____

____

____

____

____

____

____

2. *"She rises while it is still night, and distributes food to her household. She picks out a field to purchase; out of her earnings she plants a vineyard. She is girt about with strength, and sturdy are her arms. She enjoys the success of her dealings; at night her lamp is undimmed. She puts her hands to the distaff, and her fingers ply the spindle. She reaches out her hands to the poor, and extends her arms to the needy. She fears not the snow for her household; all her charges are doubly clothed. She makes her own cover-*

lets; fine linen and purple are her clothing. Her husband is prominent at the city gates as he sits with the elders of the land. She makes garments and sells them, and stocks the merchants with belts. She is clothed with strength and dignity, and she laughs at the days to come. She opens her mouth in wisdom, and on her tongue is kindly counsel. She watches the conduct of her household, and eats not her food in idleness" (Prov 31: 15-27).

Is there one verse that stands out to you particularly? Share with the group why and discuss some ways to encourage one another to improve diligence in that area.

____

____

____

____

____

____

____

____

3. Drawing upon the essay, your journaling, and the discussion, what resolution can you make this month with regard to diligence? Choose one quotation from the book or from your journal this month and commit it to memory so that you can draw upon it as you work toward diligence.

Extra Space for Journaling

OCTOBER

Patience

Dear God, I think there must be some misunderstanding.

You see, when I pray and ask for things like patience and serenity, what I really mean is that I want you to just give me those things. You know, like magic. Instant virtue! I'm not really looking to learn patience—especially not the hard way.

So when I am accomplishing something like baking for upcoming company, please do not send me a quite small person who is supposed to be napping who will instead climb the counter and use chubby fingers to snatch cranberries from the bowls and a tiny tongue to slurp on my measuring spoons.

As I smile through gritted teeth and persevere in my work, do not give me a three-year-old who has a potty accident … on my bed. Do not give me a dog that eats the garbage and then litters the deck with his leftovers. Do not arrange things so that only once I have measured and mixed all of the other ingredients for the cranberry bread and preheated the oven, I will discover that I am half a cup short of sugar.

Then, as I am sneakering small feet and bundling bodies into coats in order to go to the store, please do not allow my phone to ring. And certainly do not have it be my oldest daughter calling from the church to tell me that she just threw up all over herself, and her father is busy teaching a CCD class, and so can I please come pick her up right now?

None of this is what I was looking for. But then I have a feeling that you knew that. But you also know what's best for me, and perhaps "instant magic virtue" is not the best way for me to acquire patience.

Some days have rough edges. But I have rough edges too. I am jagged with anger, pride, and impatience. I am sharpened with thoughtlessness, hurry, and haste. I am stony. I am broken. I am rough.

And so it is on the rough days that I must pray harder still:

Smooth me, God. Even if it hurts. Rub my own sharpness against enough jagged edges to make me smooth. Soften me. Polish me. Make me shine.

—Danielle Bean

On Your Own

1. Everyone has their triggers. Ask God what sets *you* off—where you need to work on patience. Sit quietly and listen. Write what God tells you.

2. Look over your list. Think of some practical ways to counter those "impatience" triggers. Do you get enough sleep? Do you let perfection become the enemy of the good? Do you keep heavenly goals in mind, or is it always about the details for you? Enlist the help of your husband and children to support you in making positive changes toward recognizing and rooting out impatience triggers.

____

____

____

____

____

3. Who can help you? Who exhibits this virtue well and what can you learn from her?

____

____

____

____

For Further Discussion

1. *"When we ask a grace from the Blessed Virgin, we receive immediate help. Have you not experienced this? Well, try it and you will see" (St. Therese).*

When we ask for Mary's help, the only thing we can expect immediately is grace—but you have to keep asking for it, all day every day. Share about a time when you have experienced this immediate grace. Was the rest of your prayer answered right away?

2. *"Then he told them a parable about the necessity for them to pray always without becoming weary. He said, "There was a judge in a certain town who neither feared God nor respected any human being. And a widow in that town used to come to him and say, 'Render a just decision for me against my adversary.' For a long time the judge was unwilling, but eventually he thought, 'While it is true that I neither fear God nor respect any human being, because this widow keeps bothering me I shall deliver a just decision for her lest she finally come and strike me.'" The Lord said, "Pay attention to what the dishonest judge says. Will not God then secure the rights of his chosen ones who call out to him day and night? Will he be slow to answer them? I tell you, he will see to it that justice is done for them speedily. But when the Son of Man comes, will he find faith on earth?" (Lk 18:1-8).*

What prevents you from praying and asking God for the things you desire? Do you lack faith? What stands in the way of you practicing persistent patience like the widow in the Gospel?

3. Resolution: Drawing upon the essay, your journaling, and the discussion, what resolution can you make this month with regard to patience? Choose one quotation from the book or from your journal this month and commit it to memory so that you can draw upon it as you work toward patience.

Extra Space for Journaling

NOVEMBER

Gratitude

I have always thought that patience was a strong point of mine. I am slow to anger with a child. I can wait for someone I love for a very long time (just ask my husband). What I've learned, however, is that I am not patient with myself. I am eager to move on, to improve, to achieve. And in my eagerness, I miss the grace. Ann Voskamp, mother and poet, tells me why:

"Deep breathe. Love is patient. And it strikes me, an epiphany over the fry of bubbling pancakes, 'Love can only be patient when it is first grateful for what is right now.'"

It is true: I can love only when I am thankful for the now—when I embrace the present as a gift, a time and place not to be afraid of, to resist and fight, but a place to welcome as a wise bestowment from a kind Father.

Love cannot be patient when I am discontented or my fears (of failure, of bedlam) drive me to micromanage. Patience can only grow in the soil of gratitude. Lack gratitude, then lack patience, and, ultimately, lack love.

There is the checklist. The to-dos. The plan. And the neat little tick marks next to each item are proof positive of my successes. Chores finished. Lessons complete. Meals planned. Groceries purchased. Pat myself on the back. I did it. Micromanager me. But what is "it" exactly? The goal is not to conquer the list. The goal is to live my vocation without sinning. The goal is to live in love. And love is patient—even with oneself.

Ann writes that in order to be patient we must be grateful. There's the missing piece. It's not more order, or a better plan, or something else I don't have right now. It's being fully present—and fully grateful—for the now. The moment. It's not pushing us all through to the end of the day so that I can rest in the knowledge that I accomplished everything on all three of my lists. It's stopping in the moment and acknowledging its worth. Acknowledging the very gift of time.

When the two-year-old is spinning pirouettes in a dress she took from her big sister and marshmallows are growing fluffy in the noisy mixer and the big sister is wailing pitifully because she wants that dress back and I'm picking chicken for the soup (that must be made in the twelve-minutes-marshmallow-mix-time) and the phone rings and it's Danielle, I am grateful for all of it. The whole messy moment.

I will not push past it. I must slow down in it. Finish the call. Turn off the mixer. Set the soup to simmer. Wipe the tears. I cannot push on. I have to stop. We'll sort this out, my soul and me. We'll see that the list will wait, and we'll be patient with the process. We'll thank God for the pause, in the very moment of it. If I can get to grateful, he will give me patience. With myself.

I love that friend. I love those children. I love making marshmallows and making soup. I am so very grateful for each opportunity to love. The dear friend, the spinning child, and the wailing child will all know love. And so will I because he is in the moment. And over a lifetime, a lifetime of trusting him with every moment, the grace will be abundant. That's the life I want to live.

—Elizabeth Foss

On Your Own

1. As each day draws to a close, take a few minutes to make a gratitude list. If you take a few minutes to be intentionally grateful for a few minutes every evening, you will cultivate a habit of gratitude by month's end.

____

____

____

____

____

____

____

2. Take your gratitude list to God and ask him what things might be missing there. Ask God to make you more aware of the blessings for which you should be grateful.

____

____

____

____

____

____

____

3. Look for opportunities to express your gratitude in writing or in action or in words. Do you give thanks out loud to your children? Do you thank the people in the community who serve you? Make a plan to express gratitude more overtly.

____

____

____

For Further Discussion

1. *"You say grace before meals. All right. But I say grace before the concert and the opera, and grace before the play and pantomime, and grace before I open a book, and grace before sketching, painting, swimming, fencing, boxing, walking, playing, dancing and grace before I dip the pen in the ink" (G.K. Chesterton).*

Together, brainstorm ways to bring your mind back to God and gratitude during the routine of your day. Some people set their watches for pre-planned times of prayer. Nursing moms might reflect on gratitude every time they sit to nurse. You say grace before meals; how can you "say grace" all day long?

____

____

____

2. *"Put on then, as God's chosen ones, holy and beloved, heartfelt compassion, kindness, humility, gentleness, and patience, bearing with one another and forgiving one another, if one has a grievance against another; as the Lord has forgiven you, so must you also do. And over all these put on love, that is, the bond of perfection. And let the peace of Christ control your hearts, the peace into which you were also called in one body. And be thankful. Let the word of Christ dwell in you richly, as in all wisdom you teach and admonish one another, singing psalms, hymns, and spiritual songs with gratitude in your hearts to God" (Col 3:12-16).*

As we see in the essay, virtues build on one another and draw from each other. In what ways have you noticed that a lack of gratitude is a stumbling block towards attaining other virtues?

____

____

____

____

3. Resolution: Drawing upon the essay, your journaling, and the discussion, what resolution can you make this month with regard to gratitude? Choose one quotation from the book or from your journal this month and commit it to memory so that you can draw upon it as you work toward gratitude.

Extra Space for Journaling

DECEMBER

Peace

It's a mommy thing. We love to watch our babies sleep, don't we?

Unlike most toddlers, when my Gabrielle was three years old, she knew enough to get extra rest when she needed it—even if it meant succumbing to something as babyish and previously rejected as a nap.

One particular afternoon, only a few days after Christmas, she and I had a bear of an afternoon together. She wanted milk, but we were out of that. She wanted to play tea party with real cookies, but she had eaten enough sugar already. She wanted to tear through the house screaming, but my worn-out nerves couldn't take that. She wanted to play outside, but a freezing rain kept her in.

I was relieved when, by mid-afternoon, she finally gave way to the one thing she really needed: forty-five minutes of sleep on the living room couch.

She never seemed to sit quite still enough for me to get a good look at her during waking hours, so I made up for it during her impromptu naptimes. I loved to study her soft baby-like features when she was asleep. Her body warmed as she breathed steady, quiet breaths. I was always astonished by her ability to remain oblivious to the sibling chaos that surrounds her.

On that particular post-Christmas afternoon, though, when it seemed she might snooze through dinner, I decided that I should head over to the couch and try to wake her. It was dark and warm where she slept—the soft glow of white Christmas tree lights were all that lit the living room. There was the gentle sound of Christmas music playing nearby.

I leaned in close and pressed my cheek against hers. The warmth of her body enveloped me as I held my face next to hers. For just a moment, I lay there breathing with her. Softly. Slowly. Deeply.

Every moment with our children should be so peaceful and pleasant, I thought to myself.

But then, I think that maybe they all are—beneath the noise and commotion, the clutter and the pressures of daily living. Only when we slow down enough can we can see that peace reigns everywhere—just below the surface.

Those moments are there. We need to clear the clutter and take the time to treasure them.

—Danielle Bean

On Your Own

1. Think about your daily routine. Are there certain points in your day where you can cultivate a habit of stopping, reflecting, and connecting with God so that you can find the peace that lies beneath the surface? Write these down.

___

___

___

2. What tools can you use to support you in making prayer a habit in your day? Are there certain books or kinds of music that bring you the peace that can only come from drawing closer to God? Ask God to show you how you can stop and take time to beg for grace in your days.

3. Have your tools ready. Make a peaceful space for yourself—a corner with a book and a candle or even just a basket in the bathroom—where you can escape and find peace with God at any time in your day.

____

____

____

____

____

____

For Further Discussion

1. *"For pity's sake, don't start meeting troubles halfway" (St. Teresa of Avila).*

Do you meet trouble halfway? In what areas of your life do you tend to relinquish your peace to anxiety?

What are some ways we can remind ourselves that God is in charge and that our anxiety is really lack of trust?

____

____

____

____

____

____

2. *"Have no anxiety at all, but in everything, by prayer and petition, with thanksgiving, make your requests known to God. Then the peace of God that surpasses all understanding will guard your hearts and minds in Christ Jesus. Finally, brothers, whatever is true, whatever is honorable, whatever is just, whatever is pure, whatever is lovely, whatever is gracious, if there is any excellence and if there is anything worthy of praise, think about these things" (Phil 4:6-8).*

What things do you think about? In what ways do you think the things you allow yourself to read, see, hear, and talk about influence your level of anxiety? What things can you read or do instead that would encourage you and bring you peace?

3. Drawing upon the essay, your journaling, and the discussion, what resolution can you make this month with regard to peace? Choose one quotation from the book or from your journal this month and commit it to memory so that you can draw upon it as you work toward peace.

Extra Space for Journaling

SUPPLEMENTAL MATERIAL

Daily Prompts for the Forty Days of Lent

Day 1

Fast

Skip reading magazines, blogs, or anything else in the world that inspires self-pity instead of self-confidence.

Pray

Listen. God is speaking to you right now. Stop interrupting.

Give

People are more important than things. Remember that your time and your attention are more valuable commodities to your family than your accomplishments.

Day 2

Fast

Let the answering machine pick it up! Let your caller leave a message and only return essential phone calls today.

Pray

"Blessed are the ears which hear God's whisper and listen not unto the whispers of the world" (Thomas à Kempis).

Give

"Let us not be satisfied with just giving money. Money is not enough, money can be got, but they need your hearts to love them. So, spread your love everywhere you go" (Blessed Teresa of Calcutta).

Day 3

Fast

Think of a time when you knew you were a good wife or a good mom. Recreate that moment today.

Pray

When some small person tugs at your sleeve, remember that God's voice is sometimes very small.

Give

Be your real self. What does it matter if every person in the world admires you but none of it is real?

Day 4

Fast

Stop looking around you for ways to affirm your self-worth. Look up.

Pray

Don't just tell God you love him. Show him.

Give

Treat your children's feelings with the same care and sensitivity with which you expect others to treat yours.

Day 5

Fast

When you compare yourself to someone else and come up short, give thanks to God for the opportunity to grow.

Pray

Read a passage from Scripture and then sit, without saying or doing anything, for ten minutes.

Give

When you make dinner for your family tonight, make it good enough for "company." Because they are.

Day 6

Fast

Compare yourself only to the person you were yesterday, or even just this morning. Make forward progress.

Pray

The next time you go out in the car, keep the radio turned off. Listen.

Give

Clean your heart. Clean your house. Make both shine.

Day 7

Fast

Don't read blogs or message boards today. Ask God to make you aware of how much time you have gained and to show you how he wants you to fill that time.

Pray

"Prayer reveals to souls the vanity of earthly goods and pleasures. It fills them with light, strength and consolation; and gives them a foretaste of the calm bliss of our heavenly home" (St. Rose of Viterbo).

Ask God to conquer your vanity and inspire you to bring calm bliss to your home on earth so that home becomes a foretaste of heaven for your family.

Give

Go outside and play with your children. Don't just watch them, engage.

Day 8

Fast

If it doesn't build you up and strengthen you in your vocation, why read it, why listen to it, why do it, why bother?

Pray

Remember that work can be prayer too. Give God your most gruesome task today. Do it with diligence and love.

Give

Think of the kind of person your husband was when you were dating. Love and serve that person today.

Day 9

Fast

Don't rob your family of yourself in order to impress others. That's not impressive.

Pray

Give your troubles to God who is infinitely powerful and can transform them.

Give

Be Christ to your family today. Feed their minds. Fill their hearts.

Day 10

Fast

Give up your pride. "*A soul does not benefit from the sacrament of confession if it is not humble. Pride keeps it in darkness. The soul neither knows how, nor is it willing, to probe with precision the depths of its own misery. It puts on a mask and avoids everything that might bring it recovery*" (*St. Faustina*).

Pray

Go to confession.

Give

Take your children to confession.

Day 11

Fast

Don't cut corners. Even if no one will know, complete today's work thoroughly.

Pray

Light a candle. Every time you pass that candle today, offer a prayer of thanks. Don't ask for anything. Just thank him.

Give

Touch is a powerful thing. Make an effort today to touch your children: a hug, a shoulder rub, a tousled head—especially the bigger ones.

Day 12

Fast

No noise today. Turn off the TV, the radio, the iPod. Find God in the silence.

Pray

Take five minutes in the morning, at midday and in the evening to be still, silent, and alone, only asking God to infuse your soul with his will.

Give

Pay particular unsolicited attention to your least demanding child today.

Day 13

Fast

Remember the first time you had a moment alone with your first child. What did you promise him? Do that. Be that.

Pray

Begin a gratitude journal. At the end of the day, jot down five things for which you are grateful. Think upon these things.

Give

We can only expect what we inspect. For every task you assign today, follow through and before it's truly finished ensure that there is praise from you.

Day 14

Fast

Every time a child interrupts you today, stop what you are doing and look into his eyes as he talks.

Pray

"My sheep listen to my voice. I know them and they follow me" (Jn 10:27).

Give

"Kind words can be short and easy to speak, but their echoes are truly endless" (Blessed Teresa of Calcutta).

Day 15

Fast

Don't argue today. As much as possible give up, give in, give way.

Pray

Ask God to show you how weak and small you are. Open your heart to see it.

Give

When you are tempted to put on kid's TV today, pull out a stack of favorite picture books instead. Invite the kids to join you on the couch.

Day 16

Fast

Think of someone whose life you are tempted to envy and then choke out these words: "Thank you, God, for the blessings you have given to X. Help me to see my own."

Pray

Take a walk, even if it's cold or raining. (Leave your iPod at home).

Give

Think about the kind of person your husband married. Be that person for him today.

Day 17

Fast

Today, remember that you are expecting someone very important for dinner tonight. With your children, plan your husband's homecoming as if you were welcoming a king back to his castle.

Pray

"Love consumes us only in the measure of our self-surrender" (St. Therese of Lisieux).

Give

"You can do nothing with children unless you win their confidence and love...by breaking through all the hindrances that keep them at a distance. We must accommodate ourselves to their tastes..." (St. John Bosco). Do something your children want you to do with them today.

Day 18

Fast

Stop looking for encouragement and approval. Genuinely encourage and affirm someone else instead.

Pray

Take this quote to prayer today and listen to God's answer: *"Real love is demanding. I would fail in my mission if I did not tell you so. Love demands a personal commitment to the will of God" (Pope John Paul II).*

Give

Let your child choose a huge stack of picture books (use that word "huge" when you ask her to gather them). Read them all to her today!

Day 19

Fast

Don't forget that the only pedestal you need ever stand on is the one your husband and children build for you.

Pray

Persevere. *"He who does not give up prayer cannot possibly continue to offend God habitually. Either he will give up prayer, or he will give up sinning" (St. Alphonsus Liguori).*

Give

Focus on your home today. The world can find another volunteer, but your husband and children have only you.

Day 20

Fast

We're half way through. Compare yourself now to yourself when Lent began. Tweak the plan.

Pray

Insist on quiet from all your children during naptime today. Pray the Divine Mercy chaplet.

Give

Reach out to a local friend today. Reconnect.

Day 21

Fast

Don't compare or complain. Do compliment.

Pray

Ask God to make you humble and lowly.

Give

Pack a picnic and go somewhere to eat it with your children. If the weather is prohibitive, build a tent in the living room and it eat there. Sit on the ground with them. Be fully present.

Day 22

Fast

Rise a little earlier and bring your husband breakfast in bed. (If it's too late today, plan for tomorrow).

Pray

Move your wedding band to your right hand. Every time you notice the difference today, pray for your marriage. Listen to God's answers.

Give

Plan a date night for you and your husband. Make it special and make it fun!

Day 23

Fast

Clean out the refrigerator today instead of eating lunch. Pull everything out and wipe it all down. Thank God for the food he provides for your family. As you put things back, listen to God's will for you as a wife.

Pray

Give thanks for food, clothes, and shelter. Listen to God's plan for stewardship.

Give

"The poverty of being unwanted, unloved, and uncared for is the greatest poverty. We must start in our own homes to remedy this kind of poverty" (Blessed Teresa of Calcutta).

Assure the people in your home that they are wanted, loved, and cared for. Don't use words.

Day 28

Fast

You are the world to your family. Be your best world for them and only them today.

Pray

Be still and know that God is with you. Right here, right now, in the mess and under the noise.

Give

When you face a motherly crisis, remember that, way back on your wedding day, God gave you all the graces you need to handle it. Claim them.

Day 29

Fast

After a hot breakfast, take a walk. Leave the dishes, the routine, the things on your to-do list. Take everyone with you, but tell them it's a silent walk. See how long you can all just listen to the outdoors.

Pray

Set a timer to go off every hour today. Every time it rings, offer a prayer of thanksgiving for the gift of your husband.

Give

Do one of "his" chores today. Don't tell him you did it.

Day 30

Fast

Give up an extra hour before bedtime. Read with your children—all of them.

Pray

Search YouTube.com for the song "Come to Jesus" by Chris Rice. Sit quietly as you listen to and pray the song.

Give

"If people would do for God what they do for the world, what a great number of Christians would go to heaven!" (St. John Vianney).

Day 31

Fast

Call someone you have been avoiding. Offer her encouragement.

Pray

Pray in silence. *"When we pray, the voice of the heart must be heard more than the proceedings of the mouth" (St. Bonaventure).*

Give

Make toast with tea this afternoon. Invite your kids to sit at the table with you.

Day 32

Fast

After you complete any essential morning tasks at the computer for the first time today, turn it off. Do not return to the computer today unless/until it is essential for the running of your household or care of your children.

Pray

"The silence is so great that I look and do not see, listen and do not hear. The tongue moves in prayer but does not speak" (Blessed Teresa of Calcutta).

Give

"It is not how much we do, but how much love we put in the doing. It is not how much we give, but how much love we put in the giving" (Blessed Teresa of Calcutta).

With every "gift" of service that you give today, give a smile too.

Day 33

Fast

What is standing between you and greater holiness today? Rip it out. Throw it away.

Pray

Kiss your crosses. Find something small that annoys you. Embrace it; give it to God.

Give

Make your husband's favorite dinner tonight. Serve it with candles and a tablecloth.

Day 34

Fast

Be little. *"For it is part of a truly great man not merely to be equal to great things, but also to make little things great by his power" (St. Basil).*

Pray

Pray an Act of Spiritual Communion.

Give

What household job have you been avoiding? No more excuses. Tackle it today.

Day 35

Fast

Give Christ your voice today. Say what he would say.

Pray

Give Christ your heart today. Love without limit.

Give

Give Christ your hands today. Do what he would do.

Day 36

Fast

Do you have talent? Remember to give God the glory. *"The sole thing in myself in which I glory is that I see in myself nothing in which I can glory" (St. Catherine of Genoa).*

Pray

Repeat a short prayer while you do the dishes today: *"O Jesus, meek and humble of heart, make my heart like yours!"*

Give

Invite a friend for lunch. Don't worry about making the house look perfect or cooking fancy food. Be truly present to her.

Day 37

Fast

Go to bed early. Give your body the rest it needs to give all to your family in the morning.

Pray

Ask Mary to give you her heart today. Even as you go about your daily duties, keep close to Christ.

Give

Ask your kids what they like most to do with you. Do that today.

Day 38

Holy Thursday

"Simon Peter said to him, "Master, then not only my feet, but my hands and head as well."

JOHN 13:9

Call on Christ today—the same Christ who broke bread, passed the cup, and washed the feet of his disciples. Feel his healing hands. Open your heart and let him in. Let him feed you. Let him quench your thirst. Let him wash you clean.

Day 39

Good Friday

"So they took Jesus, and carrying the cross himself he went out to what is called the Place of the Skull, in Hebrew, Golgotha. There they crucified him, and with him two others, one on either side, with Jesus in the middle."

JOHN 19:17-18

Be with Christ today. Stand beside the cross and unite your sufferings with his. Compare your wounds with is and see that they are small, but give them to him anyway. Compare your strength to his and see that you are weak, but give yourself to him anyway. Walk with him, bleed with him, die with him today.

Day 40

Holy Saturday

"They took the body of Jesus and bound it with burial cloths along with the spices, according to the Jewish burial custom. Now in the place where he had been crucified there was a garden, and in the garden a new tomb, in which no one had yet been buried. So they laid Jesus there because of the Jewish preparation day; for the tomb was close by."

JOHN 19:40-42

Watch and wait with Christ today. See the dark, feel the cold, and smell the spices. Wait for his wounds to heal and his body to rise again with new life. Wait for victory. Wait for triumph. Wait for joy.

Easter Sunday

"On entering the tomb they saw a young man sitting on the right side, clothed in a white robe, and they were utterly amazed. He said to them, "Do not be amazed! You seek Jesus of Nazareth, the crucified. He has been raised; he is not here. Behold the place where they laid him.""

MARK 16: 5-6

Halleluia!
Happy Easter!

Extra Space for Journaling

Extra Space for Journaling

Extra Space for Journaling

Extra Space for Journaling

Extra Space for Journaling

Extra Space for Journaling

Extra Space for Journaling

Extra Space for Journaling

Extra Space for Journaling

Extra Space for Journaling

Extra Space for Journaling

Extra Space for Journaling